To my daughter, Athena.
May the stars be your playground.
AR

For Ava and Cassidy—I love you to the
end of the universe and back.
GF

Text copyright © 2017, 2020 by Andrew Rader
Illustrations copyright © 2017, 2020 by Galen Frazer

First Candlewick Press edition 2020

Library of Congress Catalog Card Number 2020921729
ISBN 978-1-5362-0742-2

23 24 25 CCP 10 9 8 7 6 5 4 3

Printed in Shenzhen, Guangdong, China

This book was typeset in Univers.
The illustrations were created digitally.

Candlewick Press
99 Dover Street
Somerville, Massachusetts 02144

www.candlewick.com

ROCKET SCIENCE

A Beginner's Guide to the Fundamentals of Spaceflight

Andrew Rader, PhD

illustrated by **Galen Frazer**

CANDLEWICK PRESS

The Universe

The **universe** is vast. We live among billions upon billions of **galaxies**, each containing billions upon billions of **stars**. There are more stars in the universe than there are grains of sand on all the beaches on Earth, and thousands more are born every second.

Note: Definitions for terms in boldface appear in the glossary at the back of the book.

We are made of stars. Most **elements** making up our bodies and everything around us were forged in long-extinct stars. The only exceptions are a few light elements (hydrogen, helium, and traces of lithium and beryllium) that were created 13.8 billion years ago during the Big Bang at the birth of the universe.

Gravity

Without gravity, the universe as we know it would not exist. Gravity is one of the **fundamental forces** of the universe and causes every object to attract every other one, even across vast distances. The amount of attraction between two objects depends on their masses and the distance between them (larger masses result in more gravitational attraction; longer distances result in less gravitational attraction). If you drop an object, it falls because Earth's gravity generated by all the **atoms** of the **planet** pulls the object down. (The object also pulls on Earth with an equal force.) Earth is massive; as a result, it has enough gravitational force so that large objects such as buildings and ships do not float off into space.

Our solar system began as a swirling cloud of dust, compressed over time by gravity to form the Sun and planets.

Gravity explains many things, such as why stars, planets, and larger **moons** are round. These objects are just large concentrations of lots of stuff—particles pulling toward the center of mass—and a sphere is the most tightly packed shape possible. Think of forming a snowball from freshly fallen snow: by squeezing inward from every direction, you get a nice round shape.

Milky Way Galaxy

You are here

Solar System

Our star, called the Sun, is an ordinary medium-size star in one corner of the Milky Way galaxy. Most stars are surrounded by groups of planets that form planetary systems, and our Sun is no exception.

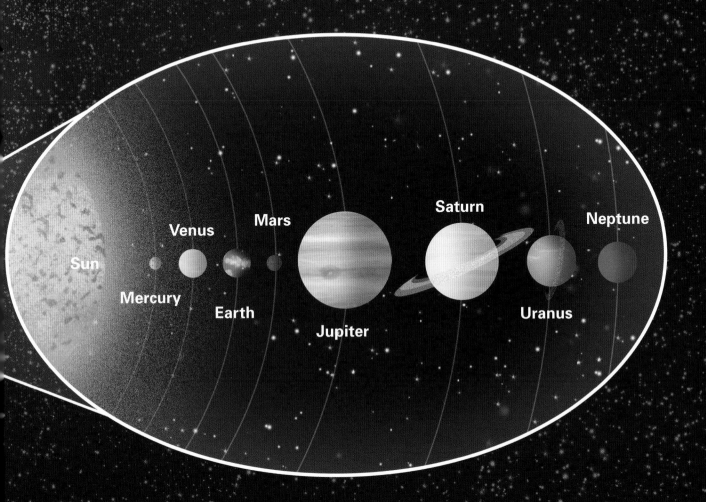

Our solar system contains the Sun, eight planets, five **dwarf planets**, hundreds of moons, and millions of smaller objects ranging from giant **asteroids** down to tiny specks of dust. Mercury and Venus are the only planets in our solar system without a moon. Jupiter and Saturn each have more than sixty moons!

Earth and Moon

Earth is a medium-size rocky planet and is third from the Sun. Part of what makes Earth suitable for life is that it's just the right distance from the Sun so that water remains liquid over most of the planet's surface (rather than being frozen or a gas). It's also large enough to have an **atmosphere**. In other words, gravity from the planet is strong enough to hold the molecules of gases like oxygen and nitrogen close enough that they don't escape into space.

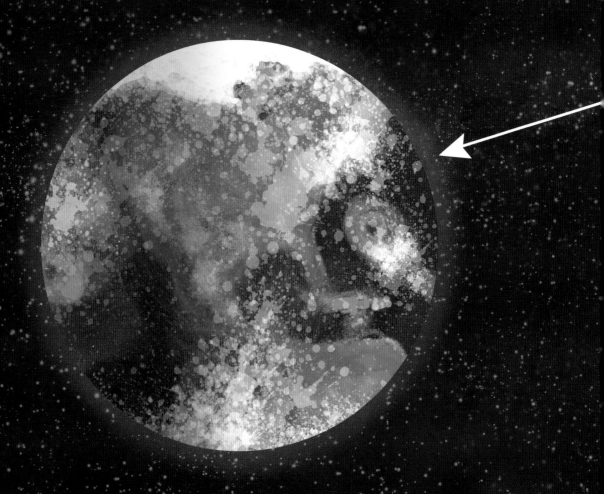

235,855 miles (384,400 kilometers)
(Earth and Moon not to scale)

The Moon is our closest neighbor in space. It is only the fifth-biggest moon in the solar system (the largest is Ganymede, one of Jupiter's moons). Scientists think our moon used to be part of Earth and formed from a giant collision when an object struck Earth and shot the Moon's material into space.

How can we get from Earth to the Moon (or anywhere else in the universe) when Earth's gravity is so strong? There is no air beyond Earth's atmosphere, so we can't use airplanes, which use wings or propellers to push against air, or balloons, which float in air, to get there. But we can use rockets!

How Rocket Engines Work

Rockets can get us into space because they do not need Earth's atmosphere to function. Instead, a rocket burns mixtures of chemicals and pushes against the resulting exhaust to accelerate forward. Since oxygen is needed to make fire but there is virtually none in space, a rocket must bring its own supply. Some rockets use liquid fuel along with oxygen that is chilled to extremely cold temperatures and stored as a liquid. Other rockets use a mixture of solid fuel and an **oxidizer**, a chemical that produces oxygen. Solid fuels are simpler but less efficient and are harder to control (once they start burning, they can't be shut off). Both types can create a controlled explosion that pushes out exhaust gases extremely fast: more than 1 mile (1.6 kilometers) per second!

**Fuel
(liquid or solid)**

**Combustion
Chamber**

Exhaust

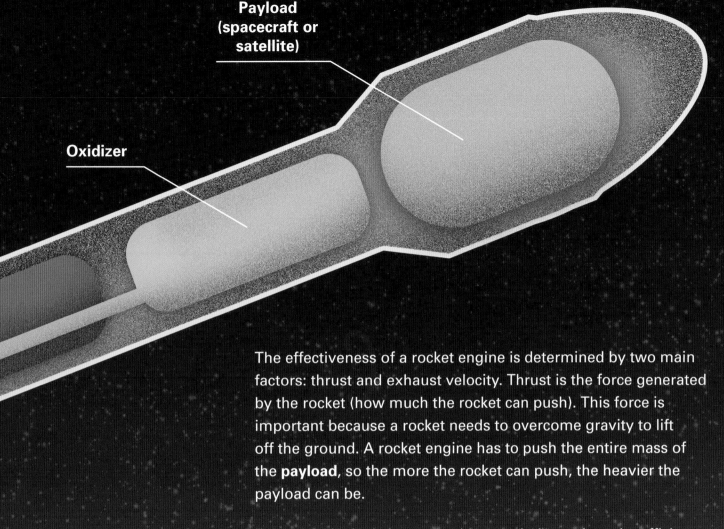

Payload (spacecraft or satellite)

Oxidizer

The effectiveness of a rocket engine is determined by two main factors: thrust and exhaust velocity. Thrust is the force generated by the rocket (how much the rocket can push). This force is important because a rocket needs to overcome gravity to lift off the ground. A rocket engine has to push the entire mass of the **payload**, so the more the rocket can push, the heavier the payload can be.

Exhaust velocity is important because it determines the efficiency of the rocket engine: the higher the exhaust velocity, the more push you get for the same amount of fuel. This characteristic is important because it's hard to carry a lot of fuel in space. In general, thrust is more important near the ground, because you have to overcome gravity until you get into orbit, whereas exhaust velocity is more important in space, where the most important factor is how far you can get on a limited fuel tank.

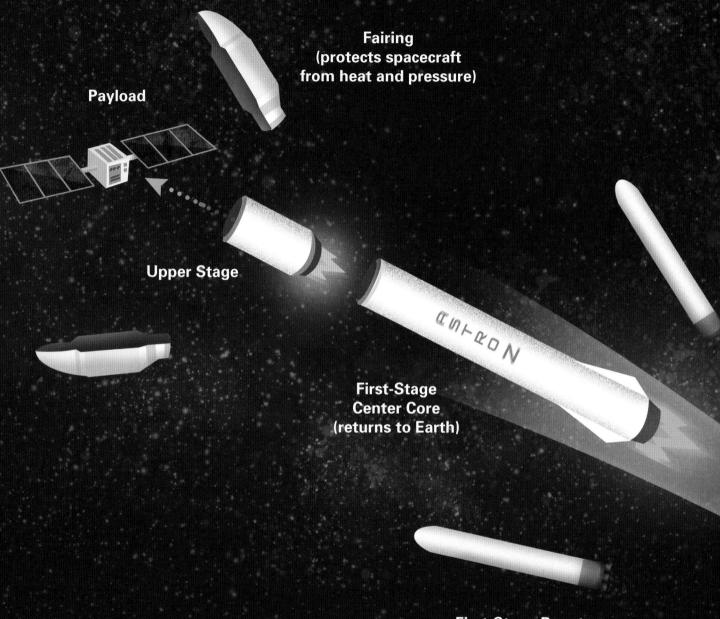

Fairing
(protects spacecraft
from heat and pressure)

Payload

Upper Stage

First-Stage
Center Core
(returns to Earth)

First-Stage Boosters
(return to Earth after using up fuel)

How Rockets Work: Staging

Getting to space is hard. It takes so much fuel that rockets are basically flying fuel tanks. Consider that a car's weight is about 2.5 percent fuel, and an airplane's weight is about 30 percent fuel at takeoff. A rocket's weight at takeoff is about 90 percent fuel. A rocket has to lift its structure and payload plus all that fuel against the gravity that's trying to hold it down. Meanwhile, it also has to accelerate to a velocity of several miles per second in order to stay in orbit, or in a path around an object.

To get to space with the least amount of fuel, a rocket must be as light as possible. One way to make a rocket lighter is to divide it into stages. Parts of the rocket that have burned most of their fuel and oxidizer can then be released, or jettisoned. Why carry an entire fuel tank when 90 percent of its fuel has been burned? Each stage has its own fuel tank, oxygen or oxidizer supply, and engine to burn the fuel. All the lower stages are shed during flight, so that only the smallest and lightest stage reaches orbit. The first stage has to push the entire rocket, but the top stage can go much farther and faster because it has to push only itself and the payload, or spacecraft.

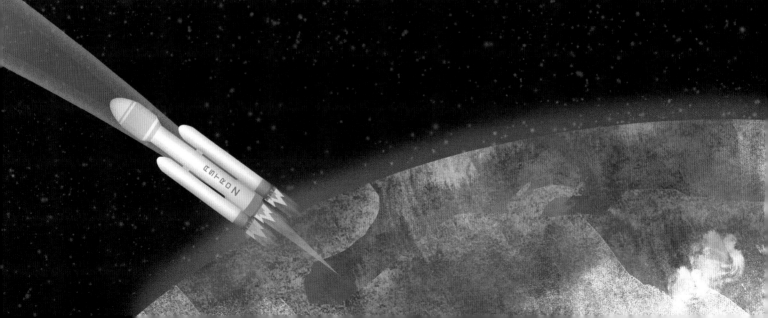

How Rockets Work: Staging

Since the beginning of spaceflight, most rockets have ejected their stages to break up in the atmosphere. This destruction is done for simplicity and to maximize performance, but it is very expensive, because it means that entirely new rockets must be built for new flights. Imagine how expensive flying would be if every time an airplane flew, all the passengers parachuted out when they reached their destination, and then the plane crashed. A brand-new airplane would have to be used for each flight!

It's possible to reuse a rocket stage, because once a rocket has used up most of its fuel and sent the upper stages and payload into space, it doesn't weigh very much. (Remember that a rocket is basically a flying fuel tank.) Therefore, a rocket can safely return without consuming much extra fuel.

With recent advances in technology, we have begun to be able to land rocket stages with precise guidance after flight, either on a special landing platform in the ocean or on land. Reusing rockets—a major step in making it less expensive to get to space—means that we'll soon be able to send more spacecraft and more people to explore and live beyond Earth.

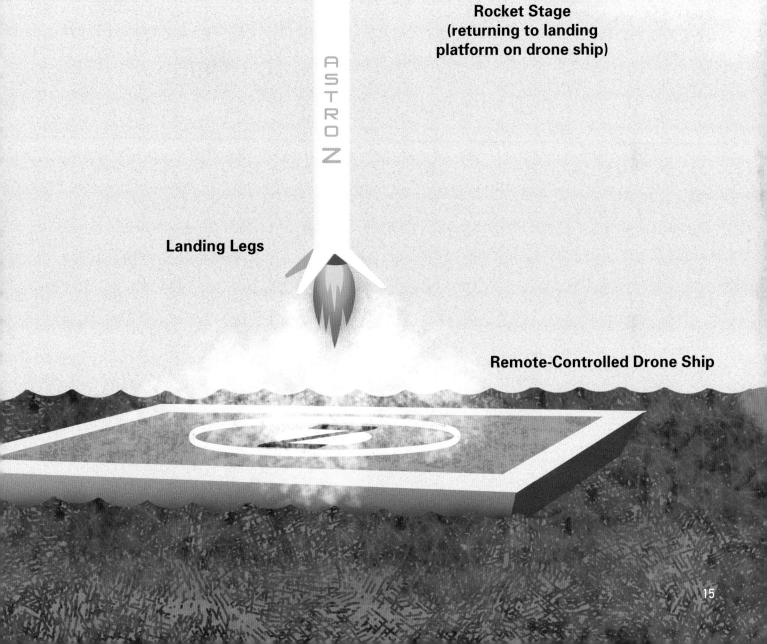

**Rocket Stage
(returning to landing
platform on drone ship)**

Landing Legs

Remote-Controlled Drone Ship

ASTROZ

Orbits

Space is very close: if you could drive a car straight up, it would take less than an hour to get there. Since it's so close, there is almost as much gravity in space near Earth as there is on the surface (around 90 percent as much). So why do many objects stay in space and not fall to Earth? It's only because they're moving sideways so fast that by the time they would normally hit Earth, Earth is no longer there.

This type of curved path is called an orbit. In orbit, a satellite is in constant **free fall**, but it's moving sideways so fast that it never hits Earth. How fast? Around 5 miles (8 kilometers) per second! That's three hundred times faster than a car or thirty times faster than an airplane. As a result of a spacecraft's being in constant free fall toward Earth, passengers in the spacecraft feel as if there's no gravity in space, even though there is.

Orbital Path

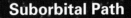

Suborbital Path

Right now the International Space Station is up in the sky above your head, orbiting our planet. If you time it right, you can even see it, as a tiny pinpoint of light, when it passes overhead. In fact, because of its inclined orbital path around Earth, the International Space Station passes above more than 90 percent of all people on Earth on a regular basis (everyone except people living very close to the North and South Poles).

Moons orbit planets, planets and asteroids orbit stars, and stars orbit the centers of galaxies, which often contain supermassive black holes, which have so much gravity that even light can't escape!

Power Generation

Imagine that we are in a spacecraft in orbit. There is no gasoline, oil, coal, or oxygen in space to burn to make energy. However, there is still light from the Sun! In fact, harnessing solar energy is more efficient in space, because there is no atmosphere, which partly blocks the Sun's rays on Earth. So our spacecraft can use solar panels very effectively to generate electricity to run computers, cameras, sensors, and other technology. In fact, a spacecraft can collect sunlight anytime it isn't blocked by the shadow of a planet or moon. During the times satellites are blocked from the Sun, they can't generate electricity, so they use energy that has been stored in batteries that were charged from the solar panels when the Sun was in view. Some spacecraft that don't need to operate for long periods of time have no solar panels and use only batteries that were charged before they left Earth.

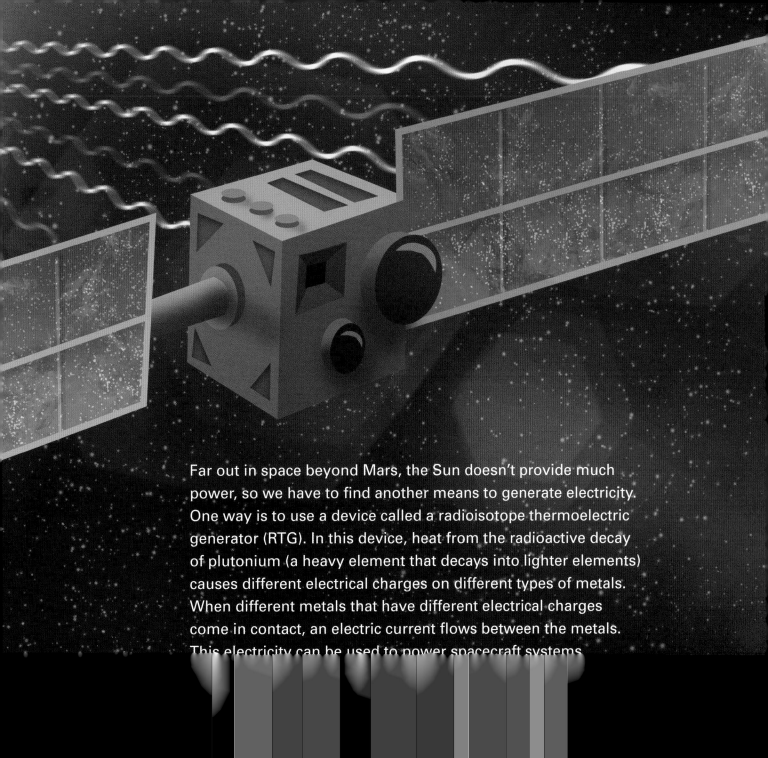

Far out in space beyond Mars, the Sun doesn't provide much power, so we have to find another means to generate electricity. One way is to use a device called a radioisotope thermoelectric generator (RTG). In this device, heat from the radioactive decay of plutonium (a heavy element that decays into lighter elements) causes different electrical charges on different types of metals. When different metals that have different electrical charges come in contact, an electric current flows between the metals. This electricity can be used to power spacecraft systems.

Thermal Control

There are three types of heat transfer: **conduction**, **convection**, and **radiation**. A good example of all three would be heating a can of water using a flame (radiation), which warms the water through the metal (conduction), after which heated water rises to the top of the can (convection).

We often think of space as cold, and indeed its temperature is only a few degrees above absolute zero (−460°F/−273°C). However, as its name implies, space is quite empty, with only a few molecules per cubic centimeter (compared with several quadrillion molecules per cubic centimeter in air). Without many molecules, conduction and convection aren't effective ways of gaining or losing heat with the exterior environment of space. Therefore, even though space is cold, overheating parts of a spacecraft is as much a problem as cooling them off, because neither conduction nor convection can be used to take heat away.

Often, the side of a spacecraft facing the Sun will become very hot, while the side facing away from the Sun will become very cold. One way to deal with this is to rotate the spacecraft over time so that the heating and cooling even out (also known as a barbecue roll). Another way is to circulate liquids through pipes that are located along the spacecraft's or satellite's framework and can carry heat to radiators, which will dissipate the heat. This system is used on the International Space Station.

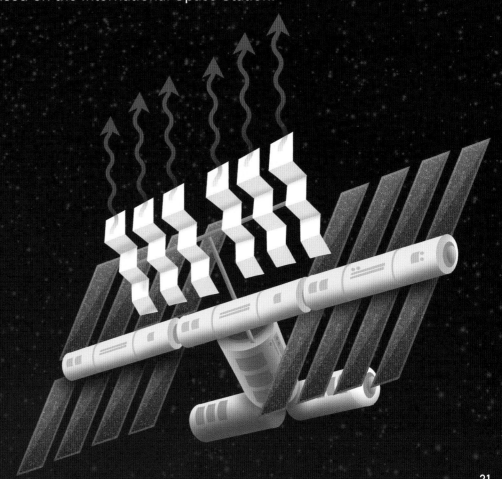

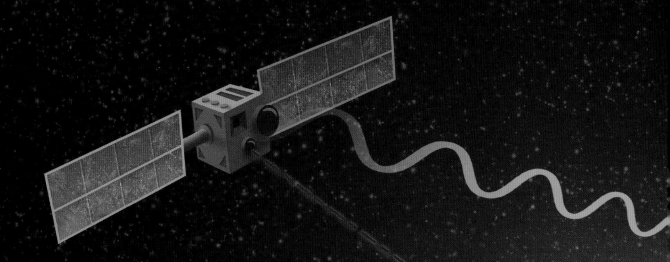

Communications

There's not much point in going to space if you can't send
information back to Earth! Spacecraft have to be able to
communicate with controllers to receive commands as well as
send pictures and data. They transmit and receive information
in the same way that smartphones send and receive calls,
text messages, and data: using radio waves. Radio waves
are invisible electromagnetic ripples of the electromagnetic
spectrum (which also includes visible light) that travel through
space at the speed of light.

How do radio waves work? At a source antenna, electric current is run through the antenna, causing the **electrons** to wiggle back and forth, creating electromagnetic ripples (in other words, radio waves). At a destination antenna, the radio waves cause electrons to wiggle back and forth in the antenna, which results in an electric current. In effect, duplicate copies of electrical currents or signals across space are created by using radio waves to transmit the information. Since radio waves decay over distance, satellite dishes are used to collect and focus weak signals to make them strong enough for antennas to detect.

It's also possible to substitute laser pulses for radio waves. In this case, a transmitter sends out laser pulses, and the receiver measures the timing of the pulses to decode information.

Guidance and Navigation

Even though astronauts still travel in space and commands are transmitted to most uncrewed spacecraft using radio waves or lasers, most rockets and spacecraft these days are able to steer themselves by computer at least some of the time. How do they do this?

Imagine trying to walk around a room blindfolded. You can still sense when you move forward, slow down, or turn to one side or the other. Like us, spacecraft have sensors that measure changes in acceleration. These sensors are called accelerometers, and they are used in smartphones to sense if the phones are moving back and forth or turning upside down. An accelerometer is how your phone can flip its screen around so that it stays upright as you rotate the phone. By using accelerometers to sense motion and knowing its starting position, a spacecraft can "guess" where it is. The guess is not always perfect, and the system's accuracy declines over time without external corrections.

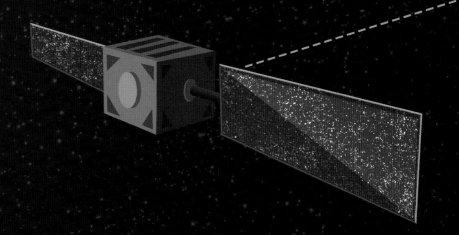

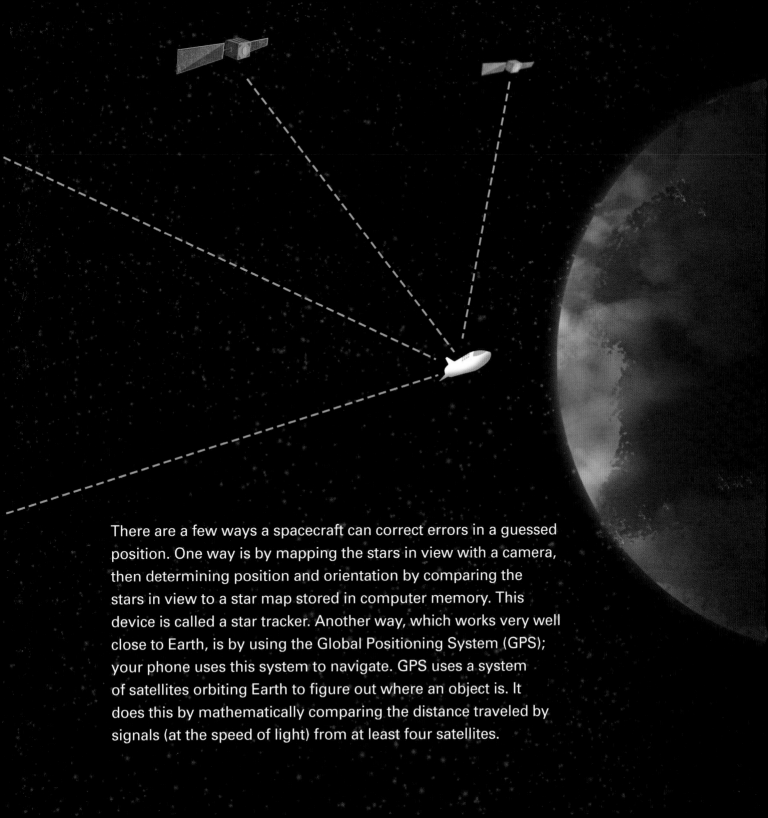

There are a few ways a spacecraft can correct errors in a guessed position. One way is by mapping the stars in view with a camera, then determining position and orientation by comparing the stars in view to a star map stored in computer memory. This device is called a star tracker. Another way, which works very well close to Earth, is by using the Global Positioning System (GPS); your phone uses this system to navigate. GPS uses a system of satellites orbiting Earth to figure out where an object is. It does this by mathematically comparing the distance traveled by signals (at the speed of light) from at least four satellites.

Going to the Moon

Let's go to the Moon! To go to the Moon, first we have to get our spacecraft into Earth orbit using a rocket, and then we'll have to perform one big engine burn that will send us on a path to the Moon. (This maneuver to the Moon is called a translunar injection.) Furthermore, to get to the Moon, we must plot a path not to where the Moon is now, but to where it will be when we get there, three days from now.

The maneuver takes a lot of fuel. The trip takes several days, so we also need to carry a lot of supplies. To carry the necessary fuel and supplies, we need a large rocket to get to the Moon, especially if we want to be able to land and then take off to return to Earth. (The supplies and the fuel to return to Earth need to be carried, too!)

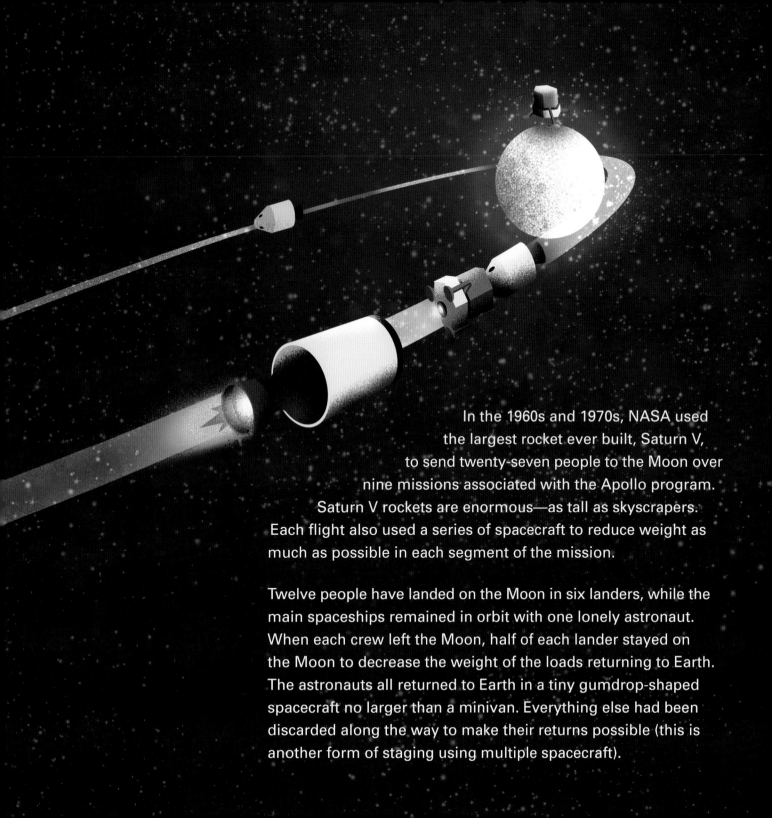

In the 1960s and 1970s, NASA used
the largest rocket ever built, Saturn V,
to send twenty-seven people to the Moon over
nine missions associated with the Apollo program.
Saturn V rockets are enormous—as tall as skyscrapers.
Each flight also used a series of spacecraft to reduce weight as
much as possible in each segment of the mission.

Twelve people have landed on the Moon in six landers, while the
main spaceships remained in orbit with one lonely astronaut.
When each crew left the Moon, half of each lander stayed on
the Moon to decrease the weight of the loads returning to Earth.
The astronauts all returned to Earth in a tiny gumdrop-shaped
spacecraft no larger than a minivan. Everything else had been
discarded along the way to make their returns possible (this is
another form of staging using multiple spacecraft).

Going to Mars

Getting to planets like Mars uses the same method as getting to the Moon, except that it takes much longer. Mars is 142 times farther from Earth than the Moon is, so it would take six to nine months to get there—and that's only when Earth is closest to Mars. Since both Earth and Mars orbit the Sun, the distance and time to travel between them varies based on their positions. Earth takes 365 days (one year) to orbit the Sun, and Mars takes 687 days. The fact that both Earth and Mars orbit the Sun means that it's much easier to go from Earth to Mars when both planets are aligned on the same side of the Sun.

To get from Earth to Mars, first we have to get into Earth orbit using a rocket. From there, we would use the engines of our spacecraft to escape Earth's gravity and send us on a path to Mars. Our path is another orbit—an orbit of the Sun. Once our spacecraft reaches Mars, we need to slow our spacecraft down to enter an orbit around Mars before we can land. One thing that's nice about landing on Mars is that it has an atmosphere (unlike the Moon), which can help us slow down while we land. Having an atmosphere also means that we can use parachutes to land (although Mars's atmosphere is less than 1 percent the thickness of Earth's, so parachutes don't work quite as well on Mars as they do on Earth).

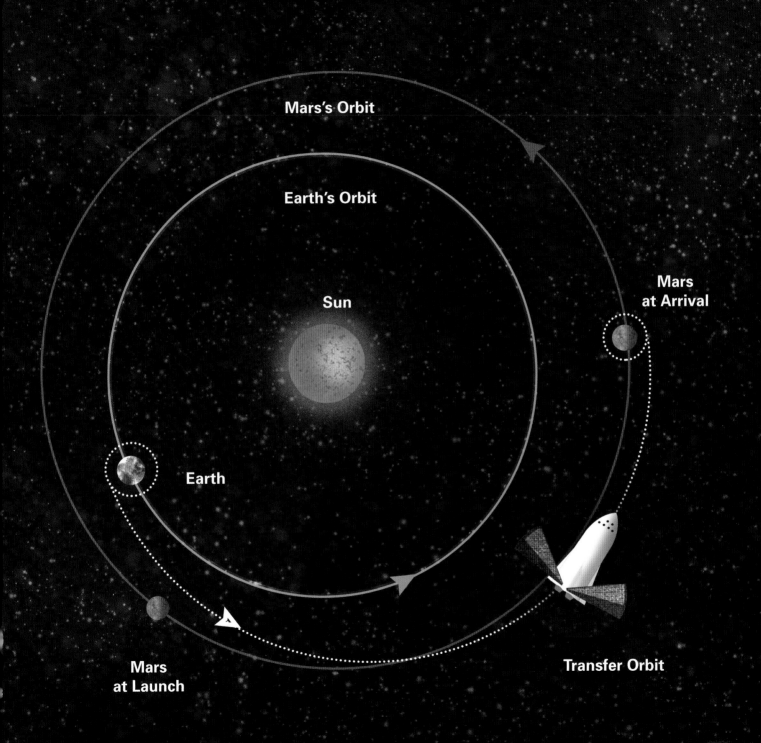

Exploring Mars

Over the years, people on Earth have sent more than fifty robotic missions to Mars; about half of these attempts have been successful. Getting to Mars is hard! In fact, there are several robots exploring Mars right now. Some of these observe the planet from orbit (orbiters), others have landed on Mars but stay in place (landers), and some have landed on Mars but drive around (rovers). The largest rover on Mars so far is called *Curiosity*, but *Opportunity* holds the driving-distance record— more than twenty-five miles in its fifteen years on Mars.

Microbes may exist on Mars, or life may have existed on the planet at one time. Robotic explorers are looking for water on Mars and searching for signs of life that exists now or existed in the past. Humans will eventually land on Mars. It's the closest planet humans could live on, but oxygen would still need to be generated (Mars's thin atmosphere is mostly carbon dioxide) and drinking water would need to be made by melting ice.

Mars has several interesting features, including Olympus Mons, one of the tallest mountains in the solar system (almost three times taller than Mount Everest), and Valles Marineris, a canyon five times the size and depth of the Grand Canyon. One of the reasons the planet has such large features is that it has only 38 percent as much gravity as Earth. This means there is less force smoothing out the planet by tugging down on tall mountains and cliffs. It also means that you could jump almost ten feet into the air!

Ion Engines and Travel to Asteroids

Using chemical rockets, our spacecraft can certainly get to Mars, but there are a few other methods we can use to travel around the solar system. **Ion** engines generate positive ions (typically positive xenon ions) and then use electric fields to accelerate the positively charged ions toward a negatively charged grid at speeds of up to 90,000 miles (145,000 kilometers) per hour—or 25 miles (40 kilometers) per second. These ions travel extremely fast out of the engine, creating thrust. Because ion engines use only tiny particles as fuel, they are very efficient for deep-space travel.

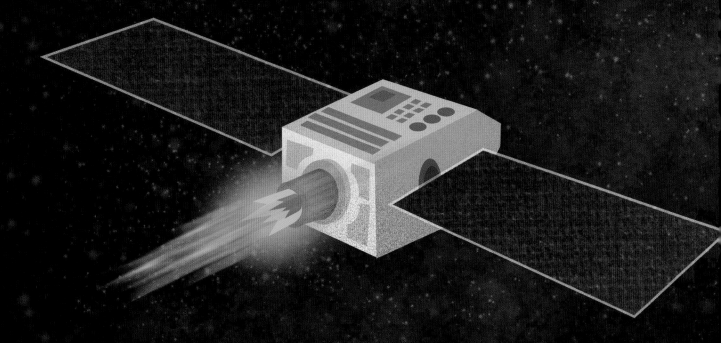

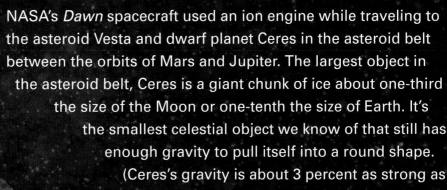

NASA's *Dawn* spacecraft used an ion engine while traveling to the asteroid Vesta and dwarf planet Ceres in the asteroid belt between the orbits of Mars and Jupiter. The largest object in the asteroid belt, Ceres is a giant chunk of ice about one-third the size of the Moon or one-tenth the size of Earth. It's the smallest celestial object we know of that still has enough gravity to pull itself into a round shape. (Ceres's gravity is about 3 percent as strong as Earth's.) But most asteroids are much smaller than Ceres and generate even less gravity. If you lived on an asteroid in the belt, you wouldn't need a rocket to fly in space— you could just jump!

Asteroids are made of valuable substances. Some asteroids are made of solid metal, containing more iron, nickel, platinum, and gold than humans have ever mined in all of history. Soon we might be able to mine asteroids for metals as well as water, rocket fuel, and minerals that could be indispensable for building distant outposts across the solar system.

Solar Sails

Solar sails are yet another way to propel spacecraft. The light and heat of the Sun are carried by tiny invisible particles called photons. On a bright day, quadrillions of photons from the Sun enter your eyeball every second. Each photon exerts a tiny push, so small that it can't be felt. But if we collect enough photons, we can propel a spacecraft. Spacecraft powered by photons use sails just like ships that sail using the particles that make up wind.

Solar sails have to be as light as possible but also very large: some might have to be miles across to capture enough photons to propel a heavy spacecraft. But since there is nothing in space to slow you down, you could eventually reach very high speeds with even a slow acceleration. Best of all, the sails use no fuel. This means that solar sails could someday be used to propel a spacecraft to another star, a voyage that could take hundreds of years.

Gravity Slingshots

Is there a way to take advantage of planetary motion? To get to planets very far from the Sun, we have to move really fast—even faster than any spacecraft by itself can go. One way to increase our speed is to use what's known as a gravity slingshot. During this process, a spacecraft gets a boost to its speed by flying close to a planet and in the direction of the planet's rotation. As a result of the planet's gravity tugging at the spacecraft, the spacecraft can move faster or change direction. The planet is very heavy compared with the spacecraft, so although the spacecraft gets a big boost, the planet is barely affected by the spacecraft's gravity. To use a planet to increase speed, the spacecraft flies in the same direction as the planet's orbital path; to decrease speed, the spacecraft flies in the opposite direction of the planet's orbital path.

Earth

Pull of Gravity

Jupiter

Extra Speed

Saturn

Jupiter

Jupiter, the largest planet in our solar system, lies beyond the asteroid belt. It is a giant ball of swirling gas and could fit 1,300 Earths inside it. It features the Great Red Spot, a storm the size of Earth that has lasted for more than three hundred years! Jupiter is surrounded by at least sixty-seven moons. Some of these moons are really interesting, such as Io (pronounced "EYE-oh"), which is the most volcanic world in the solar system, and Europa, which can be considered the largest skating rink in the solar system because its entire surface is covered by a sheet of ice. Europa probably supports an ocean under the ice, with more water than all the oceans of Earth. It may even have life swimming in its watery depths.

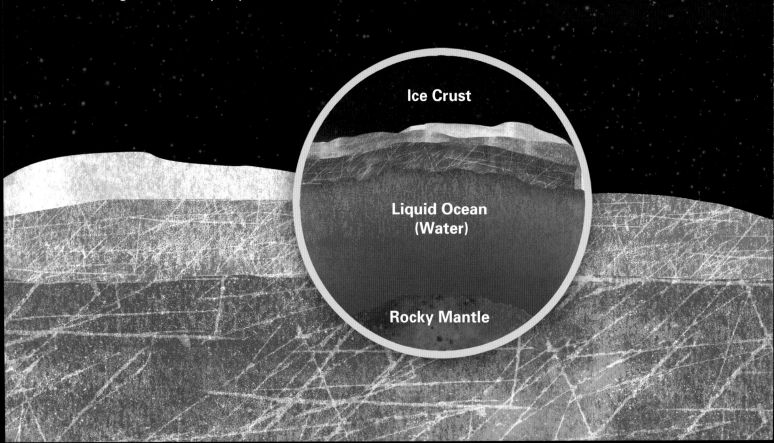

Ice Crust

Liquid Ocean
(Water)

Rocky Mantle

Several spacecraft have visited the Jupiter system, including the two *Voyager*s (1979), *Galileo* (1995–2003), and *Juno* (2016–2021). More missions are planned to the gas giant and its moons, including a lander on Europa that will look for signs of life rising through the ice from the ocean below.

Saturn

Saturn is the second-largest planet in our solar system, known for its giant rings, which range in thickness from just a few feet to almost a mile. They're mostly made of water-ice chunks ranging from less than an inch or a centimeter long to 30 feet (9 meters) long, interspersed with some small scattered rocks and other materials. Recent data suggests that the rings were formed between 10 million and 100 million years ago. Since Saturn itself formed 4.5 billion years ago, this means that the rings are a relatively recent phenomenon.

Titan

Like Jupiter, Saturn also has a mini system of its own, supporting more than sixty moons. Two of these are especially interesting and were explored in detail by the *Cassini* spacecraft, which orbited Saturn between 2004 and 2017. Enceladus is a small icy moon that supports a subsurface liquid ocean, geysers of water and ice particles trailing into space, and possibly life. Saturn's largest moon, Titan, is larger than Earth's moon and is one of the most Earthlike worlds in the solar system. It's the only other place with lakes of liquid on its surface, but Titan's lakes are filled with liquid methane at extremely cold temperatures (−290°F/−179°C). Titan also has an atmosphere very similar to Earth's in thickness and composition.

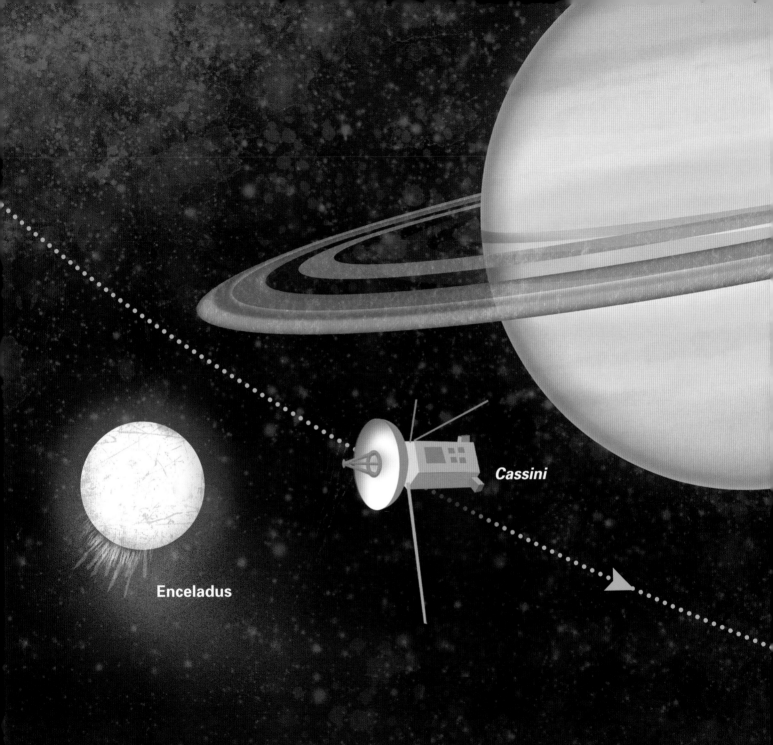

Enceladus

Cassini

Ice Giants

In the 1970s and 1980s, there was a relative alignment of the planets that made it possible for spacecraft to visit all the outer planets during the same voyage. Two *Voyager* spacecraft were launched, and *Voyager 2* took the first close-up images of Uranus and Neptune and their moons. The *Voyagers* are now traveling in interstellar space, which is the farthest any object built by humans has gone.

Uranus and Neptune are similar to Jupiter and Saturn, but because they contain more water, ammonia, and methane ice, they're sometimes called the ice giants. Each has several moons of its own. One of the most interesting is Neptune's Triton, which orbits in the opposite direction of most planets in the solar system. This orbit indicates that Triton was probably a dwarf planet like Pluto that was captured by Neptune's gravity and became a moon. Triton is also one of the few objects in our solar system with active volcanoes, but unlike Venus, Earth, and Jupiter's moon Io, Triton has cryovolcanoes, which spew out ice crystals of water and nitrogen at a frosty –386°F (–232°C).

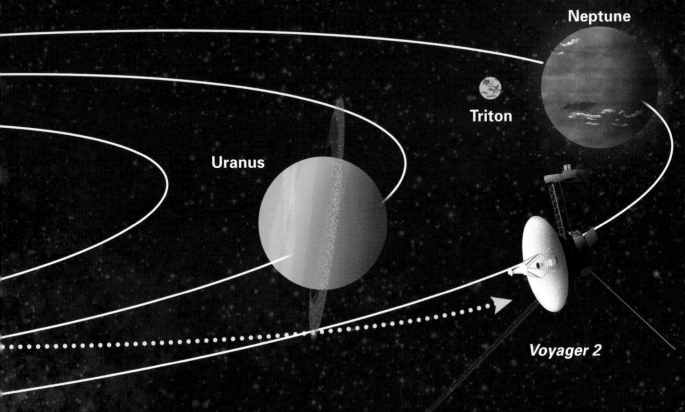

Neptune

Triton

Uranus

Voyager 2

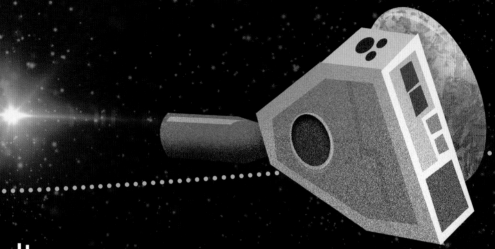

The Kuiper Belt

Beyond Neptune lies the Kuiper Belt, a region of mysterious icy worlds so far away that the Sun provides less light than a full Moon reflects to Earth. (It takes more than five hours for sunlight to reach Pluto, which lies in the belt, but only eight minutes for light to reach Earth from the Sun.) Pluto was the first Kuiper Belt object to be discovered, in 1930. Pluto is a bit smaller than Earth's moon, but it has five moons of its own, including Charon, which is half the size of Pluto itself.

In 2015, the *New Horizons* spacecraft became the first to visit Pluto, giving us an up-close look at its shape and composition. Despite being the fastest spacecraft ever launched (some have traveled faster after gravity slingshots), *New Horizons* took nine years to get all the way to Pluto! Now, having flown past Pluto, *New Horizons* is continuing to search for other icy worlds in the vast expanse of the Kuiper Belt.

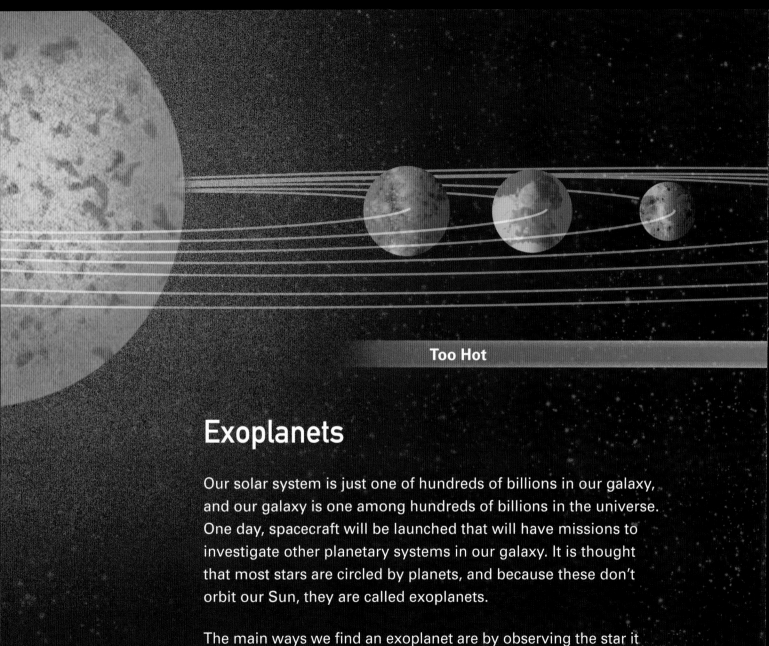

Too Hot

Exoplanets

Our solar system is just one of hundreds of billions in our galaxy, and our galaxy is one among hundreds of billions in the universe. One day, spacecraft will be launched that will have missions to investigate other planetary systems in our galaxy. It is thought that most stars are circled by planets, and because these don't orbit our Sun, they are called exoplanets.

The main ways we find an exoplanet are by observing the star it orbits and looking for slight wobbles of the star that are caused by the planet's gravity or by looking for a slight dimming of the star as the planet passes in front of it. This is a bit like looking for a fly passing in front of a searchlight on the other side of the world.

Just Right (habitable zone)

Too Cold

Many exoplanets are boiling hot or freezing cold, but at least some are the right distance from their stars such that they could have oceans of liquid water on their surfaces like Earth. We think that worlds with liquid water should be habitable—meaning they could support life. Some planetary systems are probably very different from ours. For example, a dim star might have habitable planets closer than Mercury is to our Sun. Some stars might even have several habitable planets, such as TRAPPIST-1, which has seven planets that we know of, three of which are in the habitable zone.

Extraterrestrial Life

Are we alone in the universe? We don't know for sure. Life should be able to exist on many other planets, and simple life-forms like bacteria should even be able to live in places in our solar system such as Mars, Europa, or Enceladus. If we found life on one of these worlds through our explorations of space, it would suggest that life often arises when the conditions similar to worlds in our solar system are present. The fact that the conditions for life—such as water, heat, gases, and an energy source—are found throughout the universe suggests that life should be common.

With modern technology, radio signals from Earth have now been traveling into space for more than a century. Someday, these signals might be picked up by someone. But space is really big, so it's not surprising that it may take a while for aliens to detect our signals. In the meantime, we scan the skies for signals from other beings like us somewhere out there across the vastness of space.

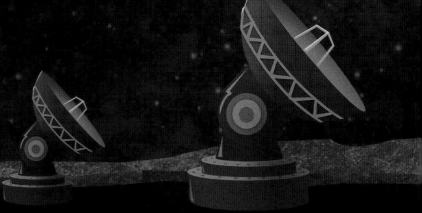

Radio Telescopes

The Future of Space Exploration

Earth is just a tiny speck in the universe. Most of everything that exists is in outer space. We'll eventually travel to other worlds in our solar system, learning how to live in space more efficiently as our technology continues to develop. We may land humans on Mars and build settlements there, using local resources such as carbon dioxide and water to produce oxygen and grow food. We might even be able to **terraform** Mars by increasing its atmospheric density to warm the planet so it can sustain liquid water on its surface. Mars would become a warm and wet world like Earth—as Mars itself was once, billions of years ago.

We may also build bases on the Moon and on many other places, like asteroids, which we would also mine for materials and water. Instead of one home on Earth, humans of the future may have many homes spread across the solar system.

Rockets and spacecraft will continue to play an important part in the journeys into space. We'll probably develop faster propulsion systems, such as **fusion rockets** or **antimatter rockets**, which could provide vastly more energy than the chemical rockets we use today. Humans have always been curious creatures, and there's a bright future ahead exploring the stars.

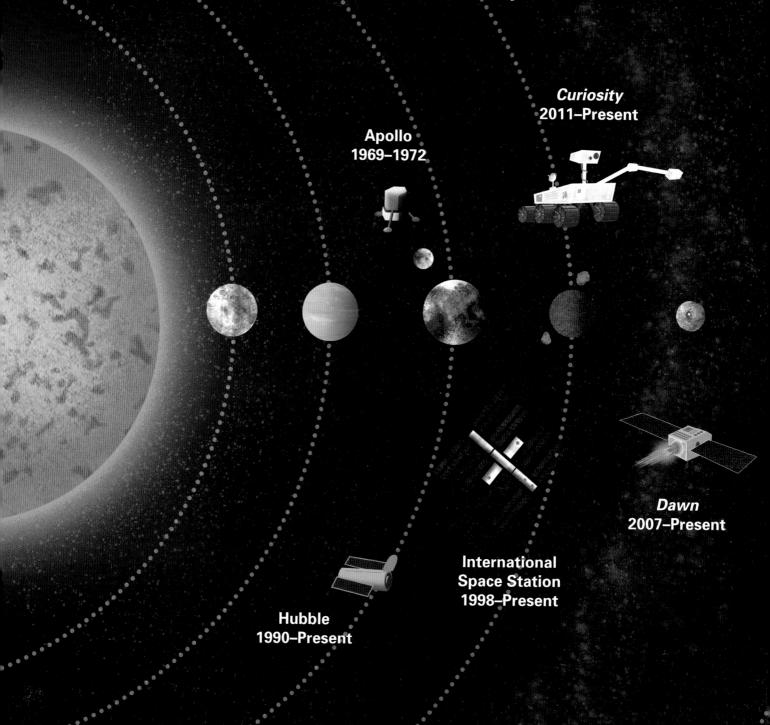

Selected Spacecraft and the Solar System

Curiosity
2011–Present

Apollo
1969–1972

Hubble
1990–Present

International
Space Station
1998–Present

Dawn
2007–Present

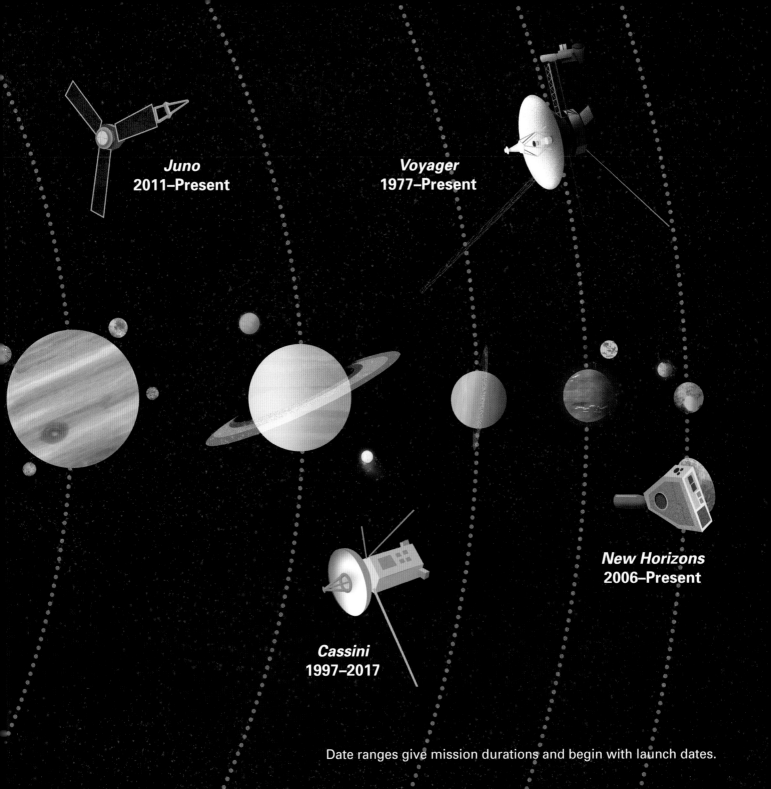

Juno
2011–Present

Voyager
1977–Present

New Horizons
2006–Present

Cassini
1997–2017

Date ranges give mission durations and begin with launch dates.

Glossary

antimatter rocket: a rocket that uses the interaction of particles to thrust itself and its payload. A particle (matter) and its opposite (a particle called antimatter) can interact, which leads to their annihilation but generates photons and other particles.

asteroid: a natural object that orbits a star but isn't a planet or a dwarf planet

atmosphere: layers of gases surrounding a planet, dwarf planet, moon, or star, held in place by gravity. Earth's atmosphere is about 78 percent nitrogen, 21 percent oxygen, almost 1 percent argon, and less than 1 percent other trace gases such as water vapor and carbon dioxide.

atoms: the extremely tiny basic building blocks of everything; made up of atomic nuclei (protons and neutrons) and electrons. There are about fifty quintillion atoms in a grain of sand.

conduction: the process of heat being carried through materials, such as if you were to touch something hot

convection: the process of heat being carried by a circulating substance, such as air or water

dwarf planet: like a planet except that it has not cleared other large objects from its orbit around a star (for example, Pluto, since there are other large icy objects that cross Pluto's orbit). In our planetary system, Ceres is the only dwarf planet inside the orbit of Jupiter, but there are at least four beyond Neptune: Pluto, Eris, Makemake, and Haumea.

electrons: negatively charged particles that, together with positively charged particles called protons and neutral particles called neutrons, make up atoms

element: a substance that is made up of the same type of atoms (atoms that have the same number of protons)

free fall: the motion of an object when gravity is the only force acting on it

fundamental forces: There are four known fundamental forces in the universe: gravity, electromagnetism, the strong nuclear force, and the weak nuclear force. These nuclear forces work at the subatomic level, holding atoms together and causing radioactive decay.

fusion rocket: a rocket that uses fusion to thrust the rocket and its payload. Fusion is an extremely energetic reaction in which two or more atomic nuclei are combined to form one or more different atomic nuclei and subatomic particles.

galaxy: a large collection of stars, planets, and other objects in the universe. Our galaxy is a medium-size galaxy called the Milky Way.

ion: a charged particle (usually an atom or molecule that has lost or gained an electron). An ion can be positively charged or negatively charged.

moon: a small natural object that orbits a planet, dwarf planet, or asteroid

oxidizer: a chemical that releases oxygen that will burn with a fuel

payload: a spacecraft carrying passengers and cargo or a satellite that is transported by a rocket. A spacecraft is a vehicle designed to fly in outer space; a satellite is a type of uncrewed spacecraft that has been intentionally placed into orbit (see pages 16–17 for a discussion of orbits).

planet: a natural object that orbits, or follows a path around, a star; has pulled itself into a round shape; and has cleared other large non-moon objects from its orbit around the star. The planets in our solar system are Mercury, Venus, Earth, Mars, Jupiter, Saturn, Uranus, and Neptune.

radiation: the only type of heat that can be carried across space, in the form of electromagnetic waves that warm cooler objects at a distance. (This is how the Sun heats Earth.)

star: a giant ball of gas that is massive enough to start nuclear fusion—the process of light atomic nuclei fusing together with intense pressure to make heavier nuclei, a process that generates energy

terraform: to transform a planet, moon, or asteroid so that its environment resembles Earth

universe: everything that exists, as far as we know (there could be additional universes as part of a "multiverse")

For Further Exploration

NASA: www.nasa.gov

Exoplanets and the Search for Life (NASA): www.nasa.gov/content/the-search-for-life

Exploration of the Moon and Mars (NASA): www.nasa.gov/topics/moon-to-mars

Exploration of the Solar System (NASA): www.nasa.gov/topics/solarsystem

Humans in Space (NASA): www.nasa.gov/topics/humans-in-space

Planets, Moons, and Dwarf Planets (NASA): www.nasa.gov/content/planets-moons-and-dwarf-planets

Canadian Space Agency: www.asc-csa.gc.ca

European Space Agency: www.esa.int

Hubble Space Telescope: www.hubblesite.org

Japan Aerospace Exploration Agency: www.global.jaxa.jp

SpaceX: www.SpaceX.com

About the Author

Andrew Rader is an aerospace engineer, author, and game designer from Canada based at SpaceX in Los Angeles. He cohosts the weekly podcast *Spellbound*, which covers topics from science to economics to history and psychology. Andrew is an avid trivia player, space and Mars enthusiast, science nerd, history buff, and incurable know-it-all.

PHOTO CREDIT: Carolyn Barnes / Alexander McGrellis

12b

FIG. 3

$$v(t) = v_0 + v_e \ln \frac{M_0}{M(t)}$$